My First Picture Book of Poetry

Collected & Illustrated by
RENE CLOKE

DERRYDALE BOOKS
New York
A division of Crown Publishers, Inc.
New York

© Award Publications Ltd. MCMLXXX
Spring House, Spring Place
London NW5, England.

This edition is published by Derrydale Books, a division
of Crown Publishers, Inc., One Park Avenue
New York, New York 10016

a b c d e f g h
Printed in Belgium.

Foreign Lands.

Up into the cherry-tree
　　Who should climb but little me?
I held the trunk with both my hands
　　And looked abroad on foreign lands.

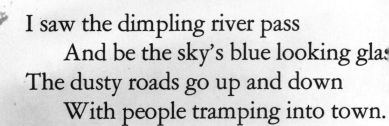

I saw the dimpling river pass
　　And be the sky's blue looking glas
The dusty roads go up and down
　　With people tramping into town.

If I could find a higher tree
　　Farther and farther I should see,
To where the grown-up river slips
　　Into the sea among the ships,

I saw the next-door garden lie,
　　Adorned with flowers, before my ey
And many pleasant places more
　　That I had never seen before.

To where the roads on either hand
　　Lead onward into fairy land,
Where all the children dine at five,
　　And all the playthings come alive.

ROBERT LOUIS STEVENSON

Where go the Boats?

Dark brown is the river,
   Golden is the sand.
It flows along for ever,
   With trees on either hand.

Green leaves a-floating,
   Castles of the foam,
Boats of mine a-boating –
   Where will all come home?

On goes the river
   And out past the mill,
Away down the valley,
   Away down the hill.

Away down the river,
   A hundred miles or more,
Other little children
   Shall bring my boats ashore.

ROBERT LOUIS STEVENSON

Ariel's songs.

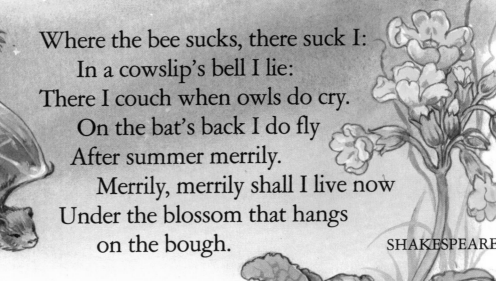

Where the bee sucks, there suck I:
In a cowslip's bell I lie:
There I couch when owls do cry.
On the bat's back I do fly
After summer merrily.
Merrily, merrily shall I live now
Under the blossom that hangs
on the bough.

SHAKESPEARE

Come unto these yellow sands,
And then take hands;
Curtsied when you have and kissed
The wild waves whist,
Foot it featly here and there;
And, sweet sprites,
the burthen bear.
Hark, hark! Bow, wow
The watch-dogs bark, Bow, wow,
Hark, hark! I hear
The strain of strutting Chanticleer
Cry, Cock-a-diddle dow.

SHAKESPEARE

The Fairies.

Up the airy mountain,
   Down the rushy glen,
We daren't go a-hunting
   For fear of little men;
Wee folk, good folk,
   Trooping all together;
Green jacket, red cap
   And white owl's feather.

Down along the rocky shore
   Some make their home,
They live on crispy pancakes
   Of yellow tide foam;
Some in the reeds
   Of the black mountain lake,
   With frogs for their
   watch-dogs,
   All night
   awake.

Down the craggy hill-side,
   Through the mosses bare,
They have planted thorn-trees
   For pleasure here and there.
Is any man so daring
   As dig them up in spite,
He shall find their sharpest thorns
   In his bed at night.

WILLIAM ALLINGHAM

The Ferry.

"Ferry me across the water,
  Do, boatman, do."
"If you've a penny in your purse
  I'll ferry you."

"I have a penny in my purse,
  And my eyes are blue;
So ferry me across the water,
  Do, boatman, do."

"Step into my ferry-boat,
  Be they black or blue,
And for the penny in your purse
  I'll ferry you."

CHRISTINA ROSSETTI

The Daffodils.

I wander'd lonely as a cloud
    That floats on high o'er vales and hills,
When all at once I saw a crowd,
    A host of golden daffodils,
Beside the lake, beneath the trees,
    Fluttering and dancing in
the breeze.

Continuous as the stars that shine
    And twinkle on the milky way,
They stretch'd in never-ending line
    Along the margin of a bay;
Ten thousand saw I at a glance
    Tossing their heads in sprightly dance.

The waves beside them danced, but they
    Out-did the sparkling waves in glee:-
A poet could not but be gay
    In such a jocund company!
I gazed – and gazed – but little thought
What wealth the show to me had brought;

For oft, when on my couch I lie
    In vacant or in pensive mood,
They flash upon that inward eye
    which is the bliss of solitude;
And then my heart with pleasure fills,
    And dances with the daffodils.

WORDSWORTH

The Owl and the Pussy-cat.

The Owl and the Pussy-cat went to sea
    In a beautiful pea-green boat,
They took some honey, and plenty of money
    Wrapped up in a five-pound note.
The Owl looked up to the stars above,
    And sang to a small guitar,
"O lovely Pussy! O Pussy, my love,
    What a beautiful Pussy you
are, you are,
    What a beautiful
Pussy you are!"

Pussy said to the Owl, "You elegant fowl,
　　How charmingly sweet you sing!
O let us be married – too long have we tarried:
　　But what shall we do for a ring?"
　　　　They sailed away for a year and a day,
　　　　　　To the land where the Bong-tree grows
　　　　And there in a wood a Piggy-wig stood
　　　　　　With a ring at the end of his nose, his nose,
　　　　With a ring at the end of his nose.

"Dear pig are you willing to sell for one shilling
　　Your ring?" Said the Piggy, "I will."
So they took it away and were married next day,
　　By the Turkey who lives on the hill.
They dined on mince and slices of quince,
　　Which they ate with a runcible spoon;
And hand in hand, on the edge of the sand,
　　They danced by the light of the moon, the moon,
They danced by the light of the moon.

EDWARD LEAR

The Lost Doll.

I once had a sweet little doll, dears,
The prettiest doll in the world;
Her cheeks were so red and so white, dears,
And her hair was so charmingly curled.
But I lost my poor little doll, dears,
As I played in the heath one day;
And I cried for her more than a week, dears,
But I never could find where she lay.

I found my poor little doll, dears,
As I played in the heath one day:
Folk say she is terribly changed, dears,
For her paint is all washed away,
And her arm trodden off by the cows, dears,
And her hair not the least bit curled:
Yet for old sake's sake she is still, dears,
The prettiest doll in the world.

CHARLES KINGSLEY

Mr Nobody.

I know a funny little man,
    As quiet as a mouse,
Who does the mischief that is done
    In everybody's house!
There's no one ever sees his face,
    And yet we all agree
That every plate we break was cracked
    By Mr Nobody.

'Tis he who always tears our books,
    Who leaves the door ajar,
He pulls the buttons from our shirts,
    And scatters pins afar;
That squeaking door will always squeak,
    For, prithee, don't you see,
We leave the oiling to be done
                By Mr Nobody.

He puts damp wood upon the fire,
    That kettle cannot boil;
His are the feet that bring in mud,
    And all the carpets soil.
The papers always are mislaid,
    Who had them last but he?
There's no one tosses them about
    But Mr Nobody.

The finger-marks upon the door
    By none of us are made;
We never leave the blinds unclosed,
    To let the curtains fade.
The ink we never spill; the boots
    That lying round you see
Are not our boots; – they all belong
    To Mr Nobody.

ANONYMOUS

The Lobster Quadrille.

"Will you walk a little faster?"
said a whiting to a snail,
"There's a porpoise close behind us, and
he's treading on my tail.
See how eagerly the lobsters and the
turtles all advance!
They are waiting on the shingle - will
you come and join the dance?
Will you, won't you, will you, won't you, will you join the dance?
Will you, won't you, will you, won't you, won't you join the dance?

You can really have no notion how
   delightful it will be
When they take us up and throw us,
   with the lobsters, out to sea!"
But the snail replied, "Too far, too far!"
   and gave a look askance –
Said he thanked the whiting kindly,
   but he would not join the dance.
Would not, could not, would not, could not, could not join the dance.
Would not, could not, would not, could not, could not join the dance.

"What matters it how far we go?"
   his scaly friend replied,
"There is another shore, you know,
   upon the other side.
The farther off from England the
   nearer is to France –
Then turn not pale, beloved snail,
   but come and join the dance.
Will you, won't you, will you, won't you,
   will you join the dance?
Will you, won't you, will you, won't you,
   won't you join the dance?"

LEWIS CARROLL

The Night-piece to Julia.

Her eyes the glow-worm lend thee,
The shooting stars attend thee;
And the elves also,
Whose little eyes glow
Like the sparks of fire befriend thee.

No Will-o'-the-Wisp mislight thee,
Nor snake or slow-worm bite thee;
But on, on thy way
Not making a stay,
Since ghost there's none to affright thee.

Let not the dark thee cumber;
What though the moon does
slumber?
The stars of the night
Will lend their light
Like tapers clear without number.

ROBERT HERRICK

Through the house give glimmering light
By the dead and drowsy fire:
Every elf and fairy sprite
Hop as light as bird from brier;

Hand in hand, with fairy grace,
Will we sing, and bless this place.
Now, until the break of day,
Through this house each fairy stray.

SHAKESPEARE
Midsummer Night's Dream.

The City Mouse and the Garden Mouse.

The city mouse lives in a house,
  The garden mouse lives in a bower,
He's friendly with the frogs and toads,
  And sees the pretty plants in flower.

The city mouse eats bread and cheese;
  The garden mouse eats what he can;
We will not grudge him seeds and stalks,
  Poor little, timid, furry man.

CHRISTINA ROSSETTI

The Swing.

How do you like to go up in a swing,
    Up in the air so blue?
Oh, I do think it the pleasantest thing
    Ever a child can do!

Up in the air and over the wall,
    Till I can see so wide,
Rivers and trees and cattle and all
    Over the countryside –

Till I look down on the garden green,
    Down on the roof so brown –
Up in the air I go flying again,
    Up in the air and down!

ROBERT LOUIS STEVENSON